The Busy Women 's Guide to ...

Salary Negotiation

How to Successfully Negotiate
Your Next Salary Raise!

Kelly Magowan

Copyright

First Printing: 2015

ISBN 978 -0-9943159-1-5

Magowan Nominees Pty Ltd
PO Box 3239, Burnley Street North Richmond, Melbourne 3121
www.thebusywomensguidetosalarynegotiation.com

All photos from: www.ingimage.com

Table of Contents

Introduction

Congratulations on purchasing *The Busy Women's Guide to . . . Salary Negotiation*. You have made a step in the right direction towards ensuring you are paid fairly for the work you do.

Whether you are currently being paid unfairly or are looking to change employers, this guide has been written to support you in your quest to negotiate an attractive salary package.

Reading this guide will give you the essential information and tools you need to conduct an effective salary negotiation. But to see growth in your bank account, you have to put what you learn into practice. So I dearly hope that you take the time to invest in yourself and your earning potential. Investing the time now to negotiate a fair salary package will provide you with an infinite number of benefits, not only financially, both now and in the future.

As a working woman, I am passionate about fair salaries for women. I have been speaking and writing on the topic for some years now.

Throughout my career, I have been fortunate to work with many amazing men and women. However, as in the past, today women remain underpaid in relation to their male counterparts. While this is gradually changing, there certainly needs to be more support to assist women in both preparing for and having these discussions.

Take heart if you are one of those women for whom the whole concept of salary negotiation is unsettling – it is completely normal. Women more so than men find salary negotiation entirely daunting and avoid it. This is to their detriment when it comes to their paychecks and bank balances – both short and long term!

Certainly employers could be more forthcoming in relation to setting up and encouraging salary negotiation meetings. However, let's be realistic this is never going to happen. The responsibility sits with working women to take charge and initiate these conversations more than we have been doing, in a way that will get results. If you don't ask you don't get!

Some of the reasons why women resist engaging in salary negotiation and career promotion conversations include; different personality types, social conditioning, overvaluing competency, over-thinking the process, lack of confidence and simply failing to act. Without acting nothing will change.

This guide provides all the inspiration you need and all the tools, tips and activities necessary to conduct a successful salary negotiation. All you have to is follow the process and start the negotiation ball rolling - be it with your current employer or a new employer.

Best wishes for your next salary negotiation.

Why Women Need To Negotiate Their Salaries

"You have to have confidence in your ability, and then be tough enough to follow through."

- Rosalynn Carter

1. Why Women Need To Negotiate Their Salaries

The focus of this Salary Negotiation book is not on equal pay for women. However, given the relevance of the subject to salary negotiation for women, it is worth noting that equal pay remains an issue across the global workplace.

1.1 Equal Pay - Facts & Statistics

Equal Pay is about men and women being paid the same for doing similar jobs. There is no avoiding the fact that, in the global scheme, women are still paid comparatively less than their male counterparts.

USA

- In 2014, women younger than 35 years of age typically earned about 90 percent of what men were paid. After 35, the median earnings for women are typically 75–80 percent.

- The pay gap has hardly budged in the last decade.

  Women face a pay gap in nearly every occupation.

*Source:http://www.aauw.org/research/
the-simple-truth-about-the-gender-pay-gap/*

UK

- In 2014, the gender pay gap for all staff in the UK was 19.7 per cent, as measured by hourly earnings for all employees. This was marginally higher than in 2012, when the gender pay gap was 19.6 per cent.

- The gender pay gap within different groups of occupations varies considerably, and has changed in different ways for occupations between 1997 and 2013.

Source: http://www.equalpayportal.co.uk/statistics/

Australia

- In 2013, the national gender pay gap was 17.5%. This has not shifted in the last 20 years. Another way to look at this statistic is that the average woman would have to work an additional 64 days per year to earn the same as the average male.

Women face a pay gap in nearly every occupation and the gap increases the higher up the corporate ladder. Women in management are paid as much as 45% less than their male peers, new government data has revealed. (The Age, February 18, 2015)

Source: https://www.wgea.gov.au/latest-news/ equal-pay-day-highlights-price-being-female

Europe

- In 2011 women on average earned 17.5% less than men in the European Union.

- Female university students expect to learn less than men once they graduate

(Source: The Economist, 'Graduate Salary Expectations Women Expecting Less, 2nd June 2011)

While females continue to become more educated and out-perform their male counterparts at high school and university, there remains a pay gap. This serves to remind us that pay inequality has little to do with intelligence and work performance. It has a lot to do with our lack of confidence!

There are obvious structural reasons why men earn more:

- Their risk profile is higher in choices of occupation – such as finance and engineering compared to teaching and nursing. The pay is higher but more volatile.

- On average, they work longer hours compared to women who are responsible for more of the home duties and the rearing of children. Men are more inclined to be working in full time roles at higher rates of pay, while, on average, more women work part time in roles with lower rates of pay and fewer bonuses and benefits.

- Women are more likely to be placed in 'lower grade' occupations than are men. Reasons for this include fewer educational opportunities.

- Some occupations that are dominated by women traditionally have been undervalued and tend to be lower paid by employers.

- Unconscious bias remains an issue.

- Women are less inclined to initiate the salary discussion and are less effective when they do so.

This is far from the whole story. Attitudes, not just of men, but also of women, play a major role in why equal pay for women remains so elusive.

1.2 Why Women Avoid Salary Negotiation

"Do one thing every day that scares you."
– Eleanor Roosevelt

Some of the issues that contribute to wage inequality will not be easily resolved and will take time before we see real changes. However, women can take control and address the imbalance in a few areas. These revolve around negotiation of salary - be that for full time or part time work, a bonus or added benefits.

Universal studies show that women are highly uncomfortable with salary negotiation. As a result, we avoid it. Even when we do enter into a salary negotiation, we don't actively seek the best deal for ourselves, but rather look for a positive outcome for both parties.

Some key facts include:

- Men initiate negotiations about four times as often as women do.

- Many women are more grateful to be offered a job and are more apt to accept what they are offered without negotiating salaries.

- Women report salary expectations between 3 and 32 percent lower than the expectations of men for the same job.

- Women who consistently negotiate their salary have increased earnings of at least $1 million more during their careers than women who don't.

Source: http://www.womendontask.com/stats.html

If the last fact does not entice you to develop your salary negotiation skills so that you have both a personally and financially prosperous career; I am not sure what will!

1.3 Common Personal Blockers That Prevent Us From Asking

"The question isn't who is going to let me;
it's who is going to stop me."
– Ayn Rand

In Kay & Shipman's book (2014), one explanation is cited for why women are less inclined than men to enter into salary negotiations can be attributed to our DNA. Their research indicates between 25-50%

of our confidence can be attributed to our DNA. (K. Kay & C. Shipman, 2014,"*The Confidence Code*")

This is not cause to give up, rather we need to make sure we take full advantage of the remaining 50-75%! It takes confidence and self-belief to ask for more money and it appears that men have more of this naturally than do women, due to genetics. Another reason is perhaps because of how girls have been brought up and taught not to be aggressive or forceful. While men are inclined to tilt towards over-confidence, women are naturally more inclined to tilt toward under-confidence! This can be rectified with some practice.

In a Hewlett - Packard (HP) study (1995), on how to encourage women to apply for more top management roles, it was determined that female HP employees would only apply for a promotion if they believed they met 100% of the job criteria. Men, on the other hand, would apply if they felt they met 60% of the job criteria. One could deduce that women only feel confident when they are perfect! (K. Kay & C. Shipman, 2007, page 21, "The Confidence Code")

Below is a list of the most common blockers that prevent women from engaging in salary discussions with their current and/or prospective employers. The majority center on the theme of lack of confidence.

- I believe I am worth more, and I don't want to seem pushy.
- I am not comfortable talking about money.
- I was raised not to ask for things – especially money.
- I am not confident selling my work achievements and the value I bring.
- It all seems too hard.
- I fear what others in the office will think.
- I am afraid of my boss.
- I fear hearing the word "NO".
- I will be embarrassed if they say "NO" to my request.
- I am afraid of losing my job if I ask.
- I have low self-esteem.

- I have not been in my role or the company long enough.
- I need to develop my skills more before I will be ready to ask.
- I don't know where to start when it comes to salary negotiation.
- I have large financial commitments and don't want to take any risks.
- They will offer me more money when they think I am worth it.
- I don't have anyone to advise or coach me.
- I am unsure of what I am worth.
- I am not good at expressing myself.
- I am unsure if I am even worth more.
- I work part time and don't want to risk losing the flexibility of my current role.
- I don't know how to start.

Activity:

Read through the list of potential blockers to salary negotiation and tick those that relate to you. Add any other blockers you may have.

- Having ticked those that relate to you, revisit these and assess how much of a blocker they really are.

- Are they really blockers or simply perceived blockers and potentially an excuse for not engaging in a salary negotiation conversation?

- For those that you consider sincere blockers, it is worth reflecting on these further and design an action plan to address them. If you don't, it is unlikely you will ever 'feel' ready to negotiate your salary package.

1.4 How We Can All Become Better Negotiators

"I learned to always take on things I'd never done before. Growth and comfort do not coexist."
– Virginia Rometty

In the next section, I have outlined a number of ways you can help yourself develop salary negotiation skills. I would encourage you to consider each point and to design an action plan to address at least one of the strategies.

1.4.1 Do Not Wait To Be Offered

To their detriment, many women are too polite when it comes to negotiating their salary. They wait for the current or prospective employer to offer them a salary, a pay increase or a bonus and then (in most instances) accept what is offered, even if they don't agree. Annual performance reviews are often tied to the pay review. All too frequently salary is not even raised in the discussion, unless, of course, you initiate it. You may simply receive a letter saying your salary is remaining the same or a small increase has been approved.

Not speaking up is foolish if you do not feel what has been offered is fair. The same applies to negotiating only on what has been presented. If there is an opportunity to bring new elements to the negotiation, such as healthcare benefits, further education or even a golden parachute, then why not ask?

1.4.2 Talk Yourself Up

Many women fail miserably at talking about their achievements with their current employers. In the instances when they do, they generally attribute all the success and effort to the team and use 'we' rather than 'I'".

Doing a great job and achieving great things at work can go unnoticed. Chances are those around you are also working hard and so as long as things are getting done, they are not overly concerned with how or who is doing the most work.

For most women, talking about their achievements or their successes does not come naturally. It is important to learn to "toot your own horn" so that your achievements do not go unnoticed by your boss. Whenever it is appropriate, you should take the opportunity to debrief your boss on your success or provide written confirmation. This additional information will help you when you decide it is time for a salary negotiation.

Activity:

Reflect on the past 12-24 months at work and document some of your achievements.

- If you cannot readily think of work achievements, refer to the Achievement Exercise in the appendix. This will assist you in capturing your achievements in a succinct way to speak with or send through to your boss.

- Having documented a couple of achievements, the next step is to broadcast them. Do so in conversations with your boss and/or via email. To make you feel more comfortable with the tone, you could say, "just letting you know that ....".

- You can also use your achievements in making sure they are mentioned in your performance review and, if they are relevant of course, in any salary negotiation discussions you may have.

> **Broadcast your achievements**

1.4.3 Learn About Salary Negotiation

"We negotiate to find acceptable solutions to problems. We start with two solutions (yours and mine) to the same problem, be it two prices, two shares, two delivery dates, two wage rates, two budget levels, and so on. When we negotiate, we search for one solution on which we can both agree. It is unlikely to be the same as either of the solutions each of us started with; if it were then somebody would have given in, which is not a negotiation. (G.Kennedy, 2004, "Pocket Negotiator")

Negotiation is something that we all do naturally in our lives and have done so since we were children (i.e. negotiating with our parents to stay up late by agreeing to eat all our dinner, negotiating daily with partner and colleagues). However, many of us find it difficult to negotiate when it comes to our salaries. It is not a case of not possessing good negotiation skills; it is more an issue of the negotiation context and subject matter. Many women are uncomfortable discussing salaries and what they are worth with current or prospective employers. The key is to learn a bit about salary negotiation (which you are doing now) and practice asking.

1.4.4 The Language You Use Sets the Scene

Use active language

The saying *"It's not what you say, it is how you say it"* is very pertinent when it comes to salary negotiation. Women tend to use language that is more passive in conversations than men, particularly when it comes to asking for something for themselves.

In the salary negotiation context, you are there to achieve a result for yourself. Therefore using powerful and active language is crucial.

<u>Passive sentences</u>, such as the following, are to be avoided:

* *"Would you mind if?"*
* *"Sorry, however I was wondering?"*
* *"If you have a moment, would it be okay?"*

Use <u>active sentences,</u> like the following, to raise the topic, set the meeting time and enter into a salary negotiation discussion.

- *"I would like to discuss X with you today?"*
- *"Let's make a time now to?"*
- *"I need 30 minutes of your time today. When are you free?"*

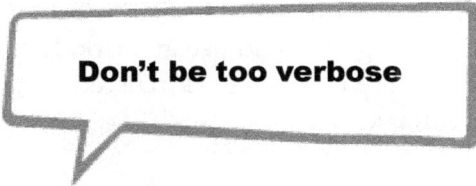

Don't be too verbose

Being too verbose in salary package discussions is an approach that women sometimes use, but that is off-putting to decision makers. Having long lists of wishes and lengthy justifications for a pay increase can result in an immediate "No". Consider your audience and their work style. If your boss is sharp and straight to the point, your salary negotiation pitch should also be sharp and to the point. Being clear and concise will more likely result in achieving the outcomes you want.

Consider a recent article in The Australian Financial Review, 'Good guys finish last in the farce that is getting ahead' (February 5, 2015). The article confirms the sad reality that confidence is valued over competence. One manager relates how, at bonus time, a procession of male, investment bankers at Goldman Sachs gave their pitch for money – sadly, no women did. In contrast, a female academic was attempting to negotiate her salary for a new position, but in a passive fashion with a waffly list of items. She was not hired.

Activity:

Reflect on the language you use at work. Is it active or passive? If you are not sure, ask trusted colleagues to give you feedback.

- If you discover that your language is largely passive, it is time to start to incorporate more active language and phrases into your workplace discussions.

1.4.5 Put Salary Negotiation Into Action

Just as most people have an aversion to public speaking, the same analogy can be made for women and their avoidance of salary negotiations. The key to becoming a great public speaker is, of course, to practice! Likewise, to improve your salary negotiation skills and the odds of increasing your salary, you need to start to put these skills into practice.

People regret inaction more than they regret taking action

The truth of the matter is - the responsibility rests with you to negotiate your salary according to your worth in the marketplace. It is not up to your existing boss or your potential new employer to take action. They are more than happy to continue paying you the same salary or to hire you as cheaply as they can – after all, that is their job. If you don't feel the skills, education, experience and personal qualities that you bring to the workplace are of value, then it is unfair to expect others to think otherwise. It is up to you to draw attention to the value and contribution that you are currently making to an organization or that you could bring to an organization, should you be hired.

We should be able to sell ourselves to our existing or potential employers and feel confident in doing so. It is up to us to take responsibility to keep our skills current and to be always learning and developing our tool kit to ensure we remain in demand. As with any purchase we make, once it is no longer of use, we naturally look to replace it with something more up-to-date or superior in quality or functionality. Fortunately or unfortunately, the same principle applies to employers.

Research shows people regret inaction more than they regret taking action. Will you regret not engaging in regular salary negotiation discussions down the road? This is particularly true if you consider your savings and envisage what it could be with those extra funds!

There have been many research experiments on the subject of "regret".

One conducted by Lewis Terman on intellectually gifted people in their 70's, he determined that 54% of regrets appeared to be regrets of inaction, whereas only 12% were regrets of action. It is important to remember, even the most successful people experience fear. The difference is that some acknowledge it and manage it as best they can so it does not hinder or stop them from achieving what they feel is important. (T. Gilovich & V. Husted Medvec, 1995, "The Experience of Regret: What, When and Why")

Activity:

Start practicing your negotiation skills today. It does not have to be at work; it could be while at the market or deciding on an expensive purchase. By practicing, your confidence will increase and better position you for your next salary discussion.

- During the next month, make a commitment to negotiate the price on a new purchase, be it a low or high dollar item.
- Make an appointment with your boss to have a salary review, particularly if it is long overdue.

REMEMBER THE FOUR ESSENTIAL STEPS FOR SALARY NEGOTIATION SUCCESS

1. Confidence

2. Powerful Active Language

3. Research

4. Practice, Practice, Practice

1.4.6 Don't let setbacks deter you

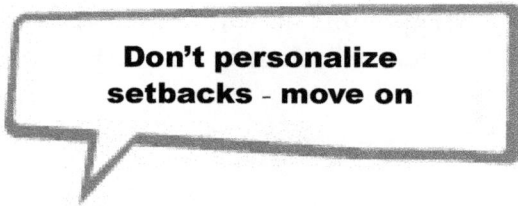

Don't personalize setbacks - move on

Not every salary negotiation is going to result in success. Even though you may have prepared your arguments and delivered your presentation beautifully, it still might not result in success. Be prepared for setbacks and try not to take it personally.

Countless studies highlight the fact that women tend to blame themselves when things don't work out the way they want or had anticipated, while men naturally blame someone else or blame the situation. Men are nowhere near as hard on themselves as women are – they cut themselves some slack and move on. This is something women can learn from men – to be kinder to themselves.

Dave Dunning, a psychologist at Cornell University, eloquently describes how women "over-personalize setbacks which undermines women's confidence". I think most of us can relate to this. He describes his male students as being able to admit when a course is tough while his female students personalize it and blame themselves and their lack of intelligence rather than the course itself. Similarly, Victoria Brescoll notes that when her female students fail to get the job they apply for, they blame themselves and view the rejection personally. Male students' reactions are to blame the process or someone else. (K. Kay & C. Shipman, page 106, 2014,"The Confidence Code")

1.4.7 Support Other Women In The Process

"If you are successful, it is because somewhere, sometime, some- one gave you a life or an idea that started you in the right direction. Remember also that you are indebted to life until you help some less fortunate person, just as you were helped."
– Melinda Gates

How often do women talk about their salary and pay increases with one another? From my experience with female friends and family, I would say rarely. I suspect it is the same for most women. While we are terrific at sharing our experiences of snaring a bargain at the shops, we are not so confident talking about our paychecks. It is ironic really that we are happy to talk about how we spend our money and how much we spend, but not how much we make. The great news is that women are terrific at sharing experiences and helping one another and are learning to share other aspects of their work life as well. The key is to begin to insert more salary discussions into these conversations to normalize them.

Activity:

We can all learn how to boost our own confidences and support other women to become better salary negotiators. From the list below, reflect on what you can do.

- Share and recommend reading; books, articles, podcasts, websites with fellow working women.

- If you are someone who has conducted successful salary negotiations, mentor other women.

- If you are a manager, initiate salary review discussions and encourage your female staff members to talk about their salaries. You may even provide a guide in how to go about the process of negotiating a salary increase.

1.4.8 What You Gain From Engaging In Salary Negotiations

> **The more regularly you negotiate the greater your bank balance!**

The most obvious benefit of salary negotiation is an increased pay packet. This creates more opportunities for you to save, invest, travel, study or do whatever else is important to you.

Another benefit of engaging in regular salary negotiations is that it forces you to reflect on your achievements and the value that you bring to the workplace. In turn, this is more likely to lead to greater confidence and self-worth.

The more women that engage in salary negotiation, the easier it will be for us all in the long term. My hope is that more women will be inspired to talk about and undertake regular salary negotiation discussions. Consider Malcom Gladwell's book 'The Tipping Point.' I would like to think that if enough women engage in salary negotiations, it would become the norm rather than something we avoid. (M. Gladwell, 2000,"The Tipping Point")

Activity:

Reflect on what you currently earn.

- Are you happy with your current salary package?

- Do you know what your salary equates to on an hourly basis?

- Do you know if you are being paid fairly? If not, it is time to do some research.

Employment Agreements

"Whatever you want in life, other people are going to want it too. Believe in yourself enough to accept the idea that you have an equal right to it."

- Diane Sawyer

Salary Negotiation Power Points

A High power points to negotiate from
* New Job New Company

B Medium power points to negotiate from
* Voluntary Exit (with counter offer)
* New Job Same Company
* Annual Salary / Bonus Review

C Lower power points to negotiate from
*Post Redundancy

2. Employment Agreements

2.1 Agreements & Payout Terms

There are many types of employment agreements: a contractor agreement (hourly or daily rate), a fixed term contract, or a rolling employment agreement. At the senior or executive level, the fixed term agreement was once popular (sometimes accompanied by a 'golden parachute'), but employers are now favoring the rolling agreement. With a fixed term contract, should the employer wish to terminate an employee who has remaining time in his/her contract, the employer is obligated to pay out the remaining time of the contract plus any and all other pertinent and applicable benefits.

With a rolling agreement, there is generally a notice period or trial period for both parties, which can range from 1 month, 3 months or up to 12 months for executive positions. This way the employer significantly reduces their payout liability.

It is not only the base salary that is considered in the payout terms. In some industries and at some professional levels, the base salary is only a quarter of the total salary package. Included could be bonuses and options. Therefore, it is not uncommon for employees who have been terminated to request a percentage of the bonus they would have received half way through the year.

When it comes to negotiation of your salary and an employment contract, there is no reason why you cannot suggest entering into a fixed term contract or negotiate the notice period. This can be done at the initial hiring or midway through your contract. Should you be exited, you may also have some room for negotiation, as employers sometimes will consider a decent payout (considered the 'price for peace on exit').

Whatever the approach, there is no substitute for extracting the best terms at the initial signing of a contract for both entry and exit.

2.2 Agreement Re-Negotiation

In a market downturn, you will find that some employers do everything they can to hold on to great employees. If you are in a position where you want to stay with your current employer but realize that the terms of your agreement no longer seem attractive, you should consider speaking to your employer to see if you can negotiate a better deal for you. This may come in the form of a delayed bonus or salary increase that comes into effect when the company reaches certain financial milestones. Alternatively, you may look to work reduced days for the same salary you are currently receiving.

Alternatively, you may be in a position where you need to re-negotiate your options or shares, as the value of them has diminished. This can be challenging in a market downturn, yet it is worth discussing if you are valuable to your employer.

The Importance Of Research And Preparation

*"Courage is like a muscle.
We strengthen it by use."*

- Ruth Gordo

3. The Importance Of Research & Preparation

> **Don't overdo the reasearch and preparation - the key is to act!**

Prepare An Agenda

Whether you are looking to negotiate a salary increase with your boss or with a potential employer, firstly, ensure that you are being realistic and secondly, that you have an agenda prepared.

List all the key points you want to cover in the discussion. Whenever possible make this a face-to-face meeting with the relevant parties as negotiations are best done face-to-face. The reason is that by being there, you are better positioned to raise and support your key points and really sell yourself. Also, it is far easier to refuse a request over the phone or via email or mail than it is face-to-face.

Research The Job Market

Advancements in technology has made it simple and easy for us to access the abundance of free salary information on the web. Search Google and you will be provided with countless salary surveys broken down by industry, profession and even State and Country.

You can search job sites to get up-to-date information about what the market rate is for someone in your profession with your years of experience. Another avenue is to talk to Recruitment Consultants or contact HR Professionals within similar organizations, or gather salary references and information from magazine articles, journals and newspapers.

Go into the meeting knowing what you are worth and with evidence to support your figures!

Prepare Your Business Case

Regardless of the economic market, current or new employers are not going to offer more money to you without justification. Having a viable business case itemizing why you deserve X salary or why your salary should be increased is still required. Show what you have done that goes above and beyond your existing role or where you have added additional value to the organization.

A pay increase generally has to be performance-based to be justified. Length of service or the fact that a co-worker is being paid more than you for the same job are not considered valid reasons.

Note: It is important to do your research and go in prepared. However don't get so involved with the research that you never feel ready to negotiate. If you are a perfectionist, it may indeed turn into procrastination!

Assumptions

We can sometimes be guilty of making assumptions about people, organizations and situations, which are not always correct. Ensure you have checked and justified assumptions before you enter into negotiations with your current or prospective employer. Common assumptions range from benefits or salaries you believe have been offered to other staff members or perks they may be receiving. Go in with your facts!

Alternatives

Always have a plan B!

Having one or more alternatives is essential when entering into any salary negotiation process.

It is important to have high aspirations; however, this needs to be balanced with the reality of the situation. Indeed, in the salary negotiation process all your requirements may be met, none may be met or some may be met. It is important to know at which point you are willing to walk away from a negotiation, and to have alternatives in place, in other words, an exit plan.

If you are working with an existing employer and requesting a salary increase, have you thought about your alternatives should you be unsuccessful? Have you begun talks with other potential employers before the meeting is arranged? You could be left hanging!

Activity:

- If you are being offered a new job, and should the salary package not meet your requirements, do you have other offers available to you?

    ○   Is this new job such a great opportunity that offers a long term financial gain that you would consider a shorter-term salary package. Or is it not what you were after?

- If you enter negotiations with your current employer and your needs are not met, what are your options? Will you leave the company? Do you have other opportunities lined up? Can you afford to be unemployed for a while? Would you consider contracting?

Remember "No deal is better than a bad deal" and you must always be willing to say no.

OTHER ITEMS TO CONSIDER NEGOTIATING ASIDE FROM BASE SALARY

Remember you are negotiating the package not just the base pay! The options are endless.

Some organisations are limited by salary bands or restrictions that prevent them from offering new or existing employees dramatic increases. However, this does not mean that they are unable to offer alternatives to straight cash increases. Be mindful of what you are negotiating. Avoid a large shopping list of items, as this can be overwhelming and considered impossible to meet!

- Sign-on bonus
- Incentive pay
- Bonus or commission
- Future salary increases (timing & percentages)
- Annual Incentive
- Equity / Shares
- Stock Options
- Discounted stock options
- Extra superannuation
- Loan to purchase home
- Car
- Loan to purchase restricted stock
- Parking
- Legal planning services

- Mobile telephone
- Private school fees for children
- Laptop
- Termination provisions
- Flexible working hours
- Golden parachute provisions
- Decreased work hours / days
- First class / Business Class air travel
- Gym memberships
- Financial planning services
- Health insurance
- Educational assistance
- Relocation expenses
- Professional memberships
- Toll Road expenses
- Reduced days same pay
- Professional clubs

Sign-on Bonus

'Sign-on bonuses' have been used widely in the USA for many years. In 2007- 2008, 70% of businesses hiring new employees used a sign-on bonus program to attract and retain staff. A sign-on bonus a lump sum payment (bonus) paid to you for signing a contract. There may be terms attached to this, for instance, if you leave within one year, you will be required to repay X dollars etc. For some people, an extra $10,000 or more upfront can be the difference between choosing company A or company B.

Only in recent years have we started to see this approach being used by Australian companies. Slowly they are beginning to see the value of such an approach across all levels of the workforce, and not just being used when making offers to those at the executive level.

Anticipate Any Problems Or Objections

*"I'm fearless, I don't complain.
Even when horrible things happen to me, I go on".*
– Sofia Vergara

There is much to be said about being positive and optimistic, but it is also important to be realistic. When entering into any salary negotiation process, be sure to consider the best and worst case scenarios. Anticipate negative responses and be prepared to respond to possible objections.

In the current market, some organizations may not be in a position to provide significant salary increases. However, there are still many industries and organizations that are strong and financially in a position to pay top dollar.

If you think you are long overdue for a salary increase, yet your current employer is not in a strong financial position at present, and you want to stay with them, you still have negotiation power. You could ask for the same pay and shorter working hours or for a salary increase to be effective when the company goes back to X amount of profit. Alternatively, you may look at options or equity if this is available.

Activity:

- Prepare a list of "what if?" questions before you enter the negotiation.

One of the most common objections you are likely to encounter when you ask for a salary package raise is variations of the following:

- "We don't have the funds right now"
- "The company is going through a rough patch, we just cannot afford it"
- "It is not in the budget"

Another common objection is about the role itself.

- "The role is banded or graded as an X, so we cannot pay you more"

Go into the discussion expecting such responses and be prepared accordingly. Remember, your employer or prospective employer always has some room to move. You will hear objections from companies with billion dollar profits about why they cannot pay you more. They can. You simply need to go in prepared to state your case. In the event they are a small employer and really cannot afford to pay you more right now, consider other negotiation items as listed in the aforementioned table.

Role Play

If you are not comfortable with the negotiation process, consider role-playing as a part of your preparation to help you increase your confidence and ensure you have covered of all the essential points. If you have a family member or friend, ask them to help you go through your agenda and presentation.

Alternatively, practice in front of the mirror or while driving your car to gain clarity and confidence in presenting your case.

Engage A Coach

If you really are not confident with your salary negotiation skills, I would recommend that you engage a Negotiation Coach or legal representative. For the small financial investment required, you can potentially receive very high returns.

The Characteristics Of A Successful Negotiator

"It took me a long time to develop a voice, and now that I have it, I am not going to be silent."

- Madeleine Albright

4. The Characteristics Of A Successful Negotiator

> **The less you say, the more power you have!**

The Perception Of Power!

Though successful salary negotiations are not entirely about power, there are some tips we can gain from those who are effective negotiators, which are two key points:

- Concealing your intentions
- Always say less than necessary

Many people are open books. We say what we feel, share our opinions, and are open about revealing our plans and intentions. This is a positive thing in our day-to-day lives, but when it comes to the workplace and entering into salary negotiations, it can work against us. When negotiating, you need to train yourself to conceal your intentions and always say less than necessary. As my father use to tell me, "It is a negotiation, not a confessional in a chapel!"

According to R. Greene (1999), power is, in many ways, a game of appearance. When you say less than necessary, you inevitably appear greater and more powerful than you are. When you carefully control what you reveal, others cannot pierce your intentions or meaning. (R.Greene,1999, "Power of the 48 Laws")

Confidence Is Key!

Research and preparation bring about confidence. If you go into a salary negotiation meeting having covered all your bases, you are inclined to come out of it with next to all of your needs being met, or alternatively you will walk away confident that it was never going to work because you could not come to an agreement based on facts (rather than emotions).

Aside from having confidence in yourself and your case for a higher salary, there are numerous personal characteristics that can make for a successful salary negotiation. Some of these include:

- Self control
- Good listener
- Problem solver
- Make suggestions
- Mention how it will benefit the employer
- Seek clarification if unsure
- Patience
- Aware that there is stress involved
- Seeks a Win-Win outcome
- Positive attitude
- Collaborative & flexible
- Quietly confident
- Realistic and makes realistic requests
- Sticks to the facts and is not emotional

Positive Body Language

Your body language can often send a stronger message than your words. Having positive body language is critical in all business situations, including salary negotiations. Your entrance, handshake and eye contact all make an impression, hence the reason for the face-to-face negotiation.

- Make a confident entrance
- If possible initiate the handshake
- Be conscious of your posture
- Hold your head up high
- Have a positive attitude
- Make eye contact
- Smile

Maintaining eye contact is incredibly important when meeting to discuss your salary, as generally it is interpreted as a gesture of trust and confidence. Nodding is another powerful gesture, indicating support and agreement.

If you can, before the meeting, practice your body language with someone you know and with whom you feel comfortable, and who will provide constructive feedback.

Activity:

Watch Amy Cuddy's TED presentation on Power Posing https://www.ted.com/ speakers/amy_cuddy Cuddy's research suggests that Power Posing naturally increases confidence and what she suggests is the perfect thing to do for a couple of minutes before entering into your salary negotiation meeting.

Negative Body Language

Body Language		Common Interpretation
Avoiding eye contact	⟶	Evasive, indifferent, insecure, passive, nervous
Scratching the head	⟶	Bewildered
Biting the lip	⟶	Nervous, fearful, anxious
Tapping feet	⟶	Nervous
Folding arms	⟶	Angry, disagreeing, defensive, disapproving
Raising eyebrows	⟶	Disbelieving, surprised
Narrowing eyes	⟶	Resentful, angry
Wringing hands	⟶	Anxious, nervous
Shifting in seat	⟶	Restless, bored, apprehensive

Effectively Conducting The Negotiation Process

*"A lot of people are afraid to say what they want.
That's why they don't get what they want."*

- Madonna

5. Effectively Conducting The Negotiation Process

Having done your research and made the necessary preparations, you should be ready to enter the negotiation process confidently. With your agenda well laid out, and your evidence gathered to support your case, you are in the best position to come to a mutually beneficial agreement. It is important to raise all your points up front in the initial meeting or discussion, rather than adding new items for negotiation as you progress throughout the process.

The negotiation process will vary dependant on whether or not you are looking at a salary increase with an existing employer or a new employer.

The environment in which the negotiation takes place is important. If possible, try to have input into the environment, which is selected for the meeting. Ideally, this should be on neutral ground. A meeting room is ideal as it puts you both at the same level and ensures no disruptions. Avoid cafes, the boss's office and open-plan spaces.

Remember, if you negotiate in a professional manner, your negotiation power is at its highest point when you receive the job offer.

Handling Salary Questions

When you contact a Recruitment Agency or prospective employer by phone or face-to-face, the issue of your current salary or your salary expectations will arise. The reason for this is two-fold: to screen out those who don't fall within the perceived or established salary range, and to give a base from which to bargain. This is irrespective of what they may be willing to pay for the right person. If you are asked to state your salary range or expectations and you do not want to disclose the information, here are a few appropriate responses:

- "I would prefer to find out more about the position, the responsibilities and expectations before getting into any salary discussions".

- "I am sure that your company (client) offers a fair compensation scale, and if we both decide that this is a worthwhile match, I am confident we will be able to agree on a salary".

- "I have researched the salaries for this level of position, and know the market value of the total compensation package is within X range".

Note: When applying online, there is often a field to enter current salary. If you must include a figure for your online application to progress, do your research so the figure you include is not under-selling yourself. Don't be shy about it. The aim is to be paid what you are worth! Alternatively, if you don't want to apply via an online system do some networking. Find out who the employer is and contact them directly. This will allow you to bypass the salary question for the initial stage of the process.

It is your decision whether or not you want to disclose your salary information during the early stages of the interview process. If you can, it is best to avoid entering into this conversation too early in the process, as it can limit your opportunity to negotiate further on. If you feel brave enough, you could ask what they are currently paying for that position but it is unlikely they would disclose this to you.

There is nothing to stop you from asking the interviewer a few questions before an offer is made to arm yourself with some negotiation power. If you are the only person they are interviewing, you can assume your negotiation power is going to be good. Ask questions such as:

- *"Can you tell me where you are in the hiring process?"*

- *"How many people are you interviewing for this position?"*

- *"How long have you been recruiting for this position?"*

If negotiating your salary with your current employer, they already have your salary information available; therefore, you could disclose the figure or items you are seeking at the beginning of the negotiation process.

Documentation & Witnesses

It is imperative that you record what has been agreed upon in a salary negotiation with an existing or new employer. Ideally, this should be done face-to-face. If possible, having a witness is also advisable.

Always try to come to an agreement in the meeting. If you cannot agree, then it is unlikely you will do so after leaving the meeting. Generally, there will be actions for each party after the meeting; make sure you document the actions that will be taken and include timeframes. Be sure to clarify if your negotiator has the authority to settle the matter, or will someone else have to give final approval. "Leave it with me" is not really a good outcome, whereas asking 'what' and 'when' will make everything quite clear.

Accepting A Salary Offer - Potential Employer

As with every step in the negotiation process, this should be handled professionally. Ensure you come across as appreciative of the offer and clarify what the offer exactly entails. Be sure to request a hard copy of the offer and ask for a few days to consider the opportunity.

Once you have made a decision, contact the existing, potential employer or agency within the given timeframe that was specified. If it is, "Yes", fantastic! If it is "No", thank them for their time and the opportunity. If it is a "Yes", but dependant on one or a few items you wish to negotiate then the negotiation process starts. This is where you draw upon your research and preparation to begin the negotiation process. It may take a few calls and discussions before you and your existing or potential employer reach a mutual agreement.

KEY FACTS TO REMEMBER

- Surveys suggest that 85-90% of hiring managers do not make their best offer first."

- "Counteroffers are generally 10-15% above the original offer."

(Source http://www.careersolvers.com/ blog/2008/02/01/166/)

Accepting A Salary Offer – Current Employer

When negotiating your salary with your current employer, it is essential to remain professional at all times. Given that you have a history with your existing employer, the situation can be more personal and therefore more emotional. As a result, it is essential to stick to the facts of why you are seeking a salary increase.

The advantage when negotiating with your current employer is that there are more opportunities to meet face-to-face and (dependant on the employer) you will have a greater insight into how much they need you and potentially be willing to offer to keep you happy. The process remains similar to accepting a salary offer with a potential employer. You have the option to say Yes or No to the offer and to start the negotiation process if you are unsatisfied with the offer but wish to come to a mutual beneficial arrangement.

5.1 Achieving A Win-Win Outcome!

According to Gavin Kennedy, "We negotiate to find acceptable solutions to problems." A negotiation requires all parties to agree on an acceptable solution to a problem, in this instance, your salary. Each party must have their needs met. Being realistic, prepared and professional throughout the negotiation process will increase your chances of securing your next salary increase, be that with your existing employer or your new employer! (G. Kennedy, 2004, "Pocket Negotiator")

You Owe It To Yourself To Act

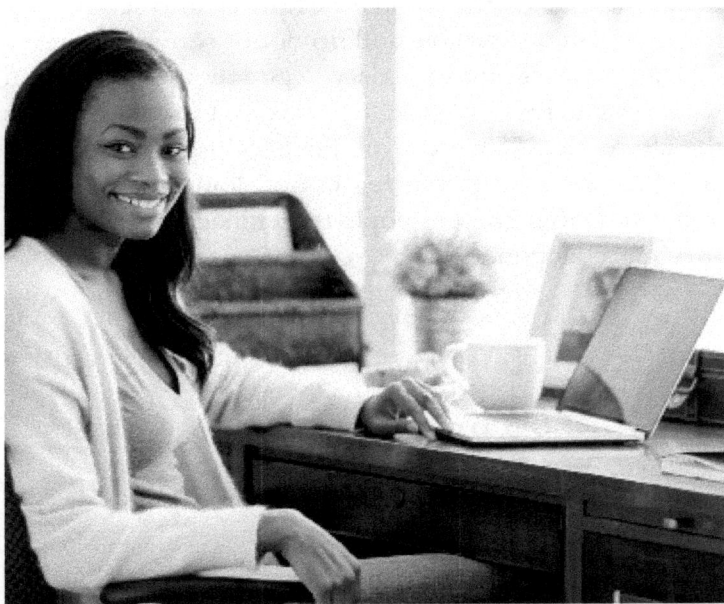

"A strong woman understands that the gifts such as logic, decisiveness, and strength are just as feminine as intuition and emotional connection. She values and uses all of her gifts."

- Nancy Rathburn

6. You Owe It To Yourself To Act

Certainly now is the time to give yourself a pat on the back for finding the time to read *The Busy Women's Guide to... Salary Negotiation*. You have taken a step in the right direction. There is however, a most important step to take – to put everything you have learned into action. Yes, it will be uncomfortable and no doubt somewhat nerve racking to enter into the salary negotiation conversation with your current or next employer. However, what is the alternative? What do you have to lose? If you don't act, chances are you will regret not doing so for a very long time. Remember people regret inaction more than they regret action.

BORROWING FROM THE L'OREAL SLOGAN, NEGOTIATE YOUR SALARY MORE FREQUENTLY, "BECAUSE YOU ARE WORTH IT".

Author - Kelly Magowan

"Nothing happens, unless you make it happen."

Author - Kelly Magowan

7. Author - Kelly Magowan

Kelly has been working in the arena of Human Resource Management, Recruitment, Career and Executive Coaching for over 17 years. Initially focusing on commercial recruitment, and later moving into corporate Human Resources working with Ernst & Young and General Electric.

In early 2003 Kelly co-founded The Clarity Group Pty Ltd, a HR, Recruitment and Careers Consultancy. Kelly sold her company share in 2006. In 2008 Kelly created Six Figures, www.sixfigures.com.au, the exclusive jobs and careers site for high salary earners to connect with $100K+ job opportunities. Six Figures was sold in 2012.

Since 2012 Kelly has been working part time at Melbourne Business School as a Careers Consultant working with the MBA students. In addition she runs her own Careers Consultancy.

Kelly has built a reputation as a thought leader in the careers space for professionals and executives. She regularly has her work published and is sought to speak at events and in the media about career related topics. One of the topics she speaks passionately about is 'Salary Negotiation for Women'. She is focussed on working with women to empower them in their worklife.

Kelly lives in Melbourne with her husband and their three young children.

8. References & Recommended Reading

Books

Frankel, Dr. Loose (2005) Nice Girls Don't Get The Corner Office. USA: Warner Business Books

Gladwell, Malcolm (2000) The Tipping Point.USA: Little Brown

Gilovich, Thomas & Husted Medvec, Victoria 1995 The Experience of Regret: What, When and Why. USA: Cornell University

Greene, Robert (1999) Power of the 48 Laws. UK: Hodder

Kay, Katty & Shipman, Claire (2014) The Confidence Code. USA: Harper Business

Kennedy,Gavin (2004) Pocket Negotiator. UK: The Economist Medina, John (2008) Brain Rules. USA: Pear Press Sandberg, Sheryl (2013) Lean In. USA: Alfred A Knopf

Stanny, Barbara (1997) How Women Get Smart About Money. USA: Penguin Books

Thorn, Jeremy (2005) How to Negotiate Better Deals. India: Jaico Publishing House

Global Salary Survey Websites

- http://www.payscale.com/
- http://www.salary.com/
- http://www.glassdoor.com

9. Appendixes

9.1 My Career Vision & Strategy

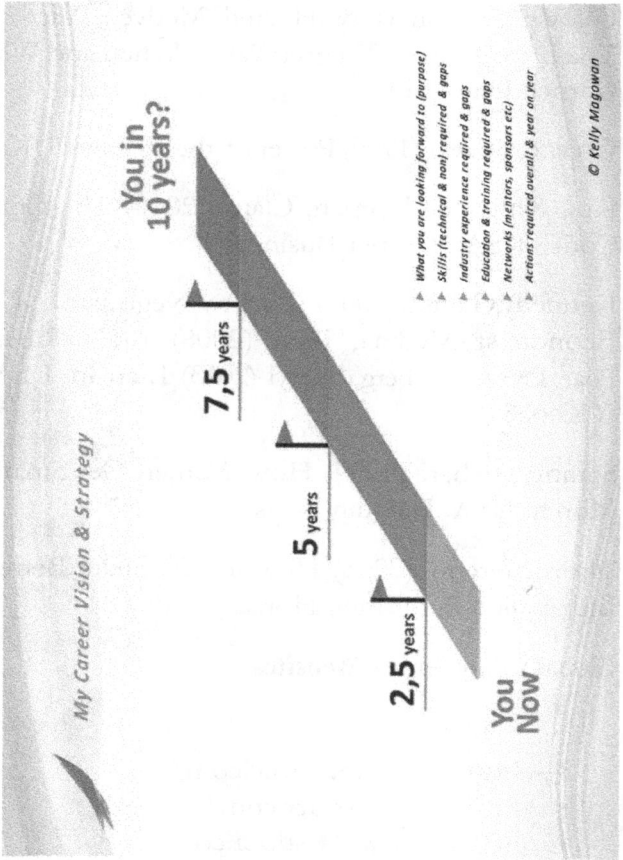

My Career Vision & Strategy

You Now

2,5 years

5 years

7,5 years

You in 10 years?

▲ *What you are looking forward to (purpose)*
▲ *Skills (technical & non) required & gaps*
▲ *Industry experience required & gaps*
▲ *Education & training required & gaps*
▲ *Networks (mentors, sponsors etc)*
▲ *Actions required overall & year on year*

© Kelly Magowan

9.2 How To Write Your Work Achievement Stories

Achievement prompters:

- Review old emails, people with whom you have liaised, meetings you attended and past performance reviews.

- Have you designed or introduced a new process resulting in a positive impact?

- Have you solved a difficult problem?

- Have you overcome adversity on a project?

- Have you had success with managing a team?

- Have you had success with training & developing staff?

- Have you received any awards?

- Have you developed a new system, a product, etc.?

- Have you designed something new?

- Have you undertaken any challenging training or education?

- Have you prepared any reports, papers, articles etc. that others were unable or unwilling to do?

- Have you saved your company or department money?

- Have you improved an existing process, product etc.?

Keep the following in mind when documenting your achievements / wins. Ensure that you are specific, that you quantify and qualify your achievements / wins. Refer to the 'CAR' Model – Challenge, Action, Result!

- **What was the challenge?**
- **What was your role, and what were the actions you took?**
- **What was the result?**

Note: Further templates and worksheets on achievement writing can be downloaded from www. thebusywomensguidetosalarynegotiation.com

9.3 Salary Package Negotiation Preparation Checklist

Action	Completed Yes / No
Prepare the meeting agenda (keep it brief).	
Research the job market for current salary data & document what you are seeking.	
Prepare the business case (keep it factual and concise).	
List your alternatives & what items you would be prepared to negotiate.	
Anticipate potential objections & prepare responses.	
Book meeting with the decision maker/s on neutral territory.	
Role play and practice of negotiation meeting.	

Notes

Notes

Notes